HORACE & RUPERT
and the Redwood Forest
Central Intelligence Agency

2008 First edition
Published by Mission Springs
Outdoor Education

2012 Second edition
Published by Bluetree 123

Written by Joan Johnson
Illustrated by Sandy Wenell Thornton

bluetree123.com

Horace and Rupert are not just ordinary banana slugs. They are banana slugs
on a mission. Their mission is to teach kids at outdoor education camp about
the redwood forest and maybe even a few things about life. Will Bentley, the
new kid from the East Coast, get through his adventures with them?

Printed in the U.S.A.

Title ID: 3830227
ISBN-13: 978-1475069297

Look for key terms that are
printed in **brown**...you'll find
them in the glossary.

Horace & Rupert

and the Redwood Forest Central Intelligence Agency

Written by
Joan Johnson

Illustrations by
Sandy Wenell Thornton

*B*entley jolted straight up in bed, gasping for air. He was crashing through the forest in the pitch black of night, running from the snarling and screeching noises of unknown creatures in hot pursuit. His eyes darted around wildly, expecting to see the claws or teeth of some hairy animal coming at him. But there was nothing except the blank walls of his bedroom.

"Whew!" he sighed to himself. It had only been a nightmare. But wait! Could this be a warning of what lay ahead for him this week at outdoor education camp?

He shivered as he realized this was the day he would be taken away from the comfort and safety of his family and thrown into the wilderness. Back at his old school in Boston, he would at least have had a group of friends to be with. Back in Boston, adults did not send children out into the wilds of the forest where unknown creatures lurked. What kind of animals lived in a redwood forest anyway? He was pretty sure that cobras only lived in places like India, but he wasn't certain. *Ecology* was not his best subject. He was an artist or at least hoped to be one when he grew up.

Bentley climbed onto the bus that morning and slid into an empty seat next to the window. He'd been at his new school in California for a whole week and still didn't know anyone. He didn't fit in anywhere. He had hoped that one of the boys would sit next to him, but the seat remained empty. He stared out the window as they drove up into the mountains, trying to look as if sitting alone was exactly the way he wanted it to be.

As the bus pulled into camp, Bentley got his first glimpse of the gigantic trees soaring towards the sky. He felt very small as he gazed up into their branches.

He was completely unaware that not so far away there were two small, yellow creatures hiding, waiting just for him.

Horace and Rupert sat among the yellowed bay leaves, watching the bus as the kids jumped off excitedly talking with friends. Rupert held the top secret file and pointed with his pencil, "That's got to be Bentley, over there, staring into the trees. Yeah, fits the description...tall, glasses, sketch book, and alone," Rupert sighed and shook his head.

"Okay, so now we've identified our target. I'll meet you at the hollow. Usual time," Horace said as he smiled to himself. He loved this part of his job working for the R.F.C.I.A. (Redwood Forest Central Intelligence Agency).

That afternoon the *naturalists* led Bentley and his class-mates into the redwood forest. Bentley, walking slowly with his sketchbook under his arm, lagged behind everyone else. His eyes darted back and forth into the trees, expecting something ferocious to jump out from behind a rock.

"Come on, Bentley, we're almost there," Keith, one of the naturalists, called back. Bentley looked up ahead and saw his classmates disappearing into a dark tunnel-like hole through the trunk of a large tree. "What if there are poisonous snakes lurking inside?" he wondered to himself.

Bentley nervously entered the tree, squinting into the dark corners along the ground. He jumped at the sight of two long, yellow, slimy things. But wait, he thought. They were too small to be snakes! He bent down to have a closer look. That's when it happened...POOF! He found himself staring into the eyes of two very strange creatures.

"Aaaaahh!!!" he screamed and started to run. What was hap-pening to him? He looked back at the entrance, but it was so far away and had grown to an enormous size. Bentley's head spun back around. Were the creatures going to gobble him up in one big gulp? His eyes grew big in amazement. Somehow, these creatures looked a lot like the yellow slimy things he had just bent down to see. Only now they were huge. Was he having another crazy nightmare??

"Calm down, kid, calm down. No one's going to hurt you!" Now the creatures were talking to him!! Bentley backed up against the inside edge of the tree. He crouched down with

his arm over his face, yelling,
"Don't eat me! Don't eat me!"

"Yuk!" Rupert grimaced as he spat on the ground, "Eat YOU?
You're making my stomach all queasy. We don't eat kids.
Mmmm, but can you catch that aroma of something rotting
somewhere? Now that smells mighty tasty!"

"Yuk!" Now Bentley felt sick. "Who ARE you guys?" he shouted.

Horace raised his eyebrows in shock and dismay. "We're
banana slugs!! What else would we be? C'mon kid, relax!
We've got lots to talk to you about, so let's get started."

"St-st-st-started? Started on what?" Bentley asked in a frightened voice. "What's happening and where am I?"

"Slippery slime trails! Look around you kid. You're in a redwood forest." Horace exclaimed.

"Yeah, but…but I didn't know that there were slugs the size of kids in a redwood forest!"

"Slugs the size of kids? What are you talking about? We aren't your size… you've been shrunk down to OUR size!"

Bentley shook his head slowly, his eyes growing wide in disbelief.

"We don't have all day you know. Can we get back to the redwood forest?" Rupert asked.

Not waiting for a reply, Rupert went on, "Redwood trees are some of the oldest and biggest living things on the planet. Why, there's a tree not far from here that's as tall as a football field is long, and it's 2000 years old. Redwood trees grow here in this *habitat* because the climate is just right for them."

"Habitat? What's that?" Bentley asked, his interest beginning to grow.

"A habitat is a place where an *organism* lives and gets what it needs to survive. Let's go outside." Rupert motioned to Bentley to follow them. Bentley eyed them both cautiously, then followed them out of the tree.

Outside the ground was damp. He looked up. The redwood tree went on forever. He could barely see where it disappeared into the fog.

"Okay, kid, now pay attention! It's very important that you understand how the redwood forest *ecosystem* works," Horace said.

"Wait! How can I understand anything if you keep using words I don't know?" Bentley threw up his hands in exasperation. "What's an ecosystem, and how am I going to remember all of these things?"

"Slippery slime trails!" Rupert exclaimed, as he nudged Bentley and pointed to his sketchbook. "Aren't you an artist? You could start by

drawing this redwood tree here and add the details as we go."

Bentley dug out the small box of colored pencils he kept in his backpack and began drawing.

Poison Oak

Bay

Douglas Fir

Producers

Acorns

Redwood Sorrel

Tan Oak

Redwood

Bracken Fern

Sword Fern

"Now where were we? Oh yeah, the redwood forest ecosystem. So, an ecosystem is a *community*..." Horace began.

Bentley drew as Horace and Rupert took turns explaining things. "*Producers* make their own food. Plants are producers. They make their food through an unbelievable and amazing process called *photosynthesis*. In this process they use water, the sun's energy, minerals in the soil and the carbon dioxide we breathe out," Rupert declared.

"*Consumers* eat producers and other animals..." Horace continued.

"And, we slugs are *decomposers*, the most important part of the ecosystem," Rupert announced proudly. "We break things down to put nutrients back into the soil for the producers to use and provide food for the consumers. We keep the entire cycle going. Without us, there would be no redwood forest!"

"Wow, will you look at this, Horace? The kid really has talent."

Horace grew very serious. "One more very important word, kid, *niche*. A niche is what each organism provides for the benefit of the whole community."

"So, now do you get it? We're a community and we all have our own part to play. We need each other." Horace stared straight into Bentley's eyes. "You know it's the same for human communities too."

"What do you mean?" Bentley asked.

"Every person has their own niche," Rupert exclaimed. "You, for instance, are good at observing. You see the details. So when you sketch something, like the redwood forest habitat, you allow others to understand what they are seeing in new and different ways. That's what a niche is for, to help others in your community."

Bentley's forehead wrinkled as he looked more closely at his sketch. Niches, habitats, communities… it was all a jumble in his head. He closed his eyes, trying to think harder and... POOF! There he was, back to his normal size, in the hollow of the redwood tree.

"Hey buddy, I've been waiting for you!" Kevin, one of the naturalists, was saying. Bentley looked up as Kevin's face came poking back through the hollowed out tunnel in the tree. "Let's catch up to the rest of the class. Are you okay?"

Bentley could only stare and say, "I g-guess so," in a small shaky voice. Kevin put his hand on Bentley's shoulder as they joined his classmates.

Bentley sat down on a fallen log next to a boy he recognized from his class. He sat there in a daze. New ideas were exploding and crashing into one another like popcorn in his brain. He looked down at his sketchbook, but his thoughts were interrupted by the feeling of someone leaning over his shoulder.

"Where did you get this?" Amber, one of the naturalists, asked in surprise, pointing at his drawing.

"I, um…drew it?" Bentley replied doubtfully. Had he really been talking with banana slugs just a few minutes ago?

"Mind if I borrow it for a moment?" she asked.

"Okay," Bentley whispered uncertainly.

Amber looked over to the other naturalist, Stephanie, who was teaching the class about habitats, and pointed at the sketchbook.

"Check this out. Bentley drew it." Amber smiled.

Stephanie's eyes brightened. "This is exactly what I've been trying to say." She held the drawing up for the class to see.

"Whoa. That's so cool!" the boy next to Bentley blurted out. "Now I can see what you've been saying. A niche is the part each thing plays in the community where it lives."

Maybe I do have a niche, Bentley thought.

Clouds

Sun Energy

Birds are consumers – get energy from plants and animals

Fog

Plants catch Sun's energy and turn it into food and oxygen

Animals are consumers – they eat food made by producers

Moisture from the fog nourishes the Redwoods

Consumers get energy from other animals

Decomposers eat the by-products from producers and consumers, like dead leaves and trees

Horace was right, everyone and everything has a role to play that benefits their community. We are all important. Bentley began to get excited as he thought of ways he could communicate this through his drawings.

The boy next to him on the log leaned toward Bentley and said, "My name's Jeremy. Aren't you the new kid from Boston?"

"Yeah," Bentley replied.

"Hey, wanna hang out this week?"

"Sounds great!" Bentley said.

Just then they heard Cassie's excited voice. "Hey look! There are two banana slugs over here!"

"Wow. You really have sharp eyes, Cassie," Lorraine praised as she turned towards the class. "Does anyone want to join the Banana Slug Club by putting one on your nose?"

Jeremy elbowed his new friend, "Come on, Bentley, let's do it."

15

Bentley and Jeremy both jumped up and ran to where Lorraine and the kids stood. As Lorraine laid the slug gently across Bentley's nose, he noticed something strange. The slug was winking at him. He looked closer. Slippery slime trails! It was Horace! And he appeared to be laughing. Bentley grinned and winked back.

He quickly glanced over at Jeremy and there was Rupert on Jeremy's nose, waving and trying to leap in the air. But, of course, it was impossible for Rupert to leap because he was a *gastropod*. Bentley gave a slight nod of his head to Rupert as his smile grew bigger.

Their classmates gathered around them both and began cheering. Bentley could no longer contain himself, and his smile bubbled up into laughter.

At the end of the week, as Bentley sat on the bus heading for home, some curious questions suddenly popped into his head. Who were Horace and Rupert anyway? Did they plan a new adventure each week for some poor, unsuspecting student? His face lit up as he chuckled to himself, "I certainly hope so!"

Cool Slug Facts

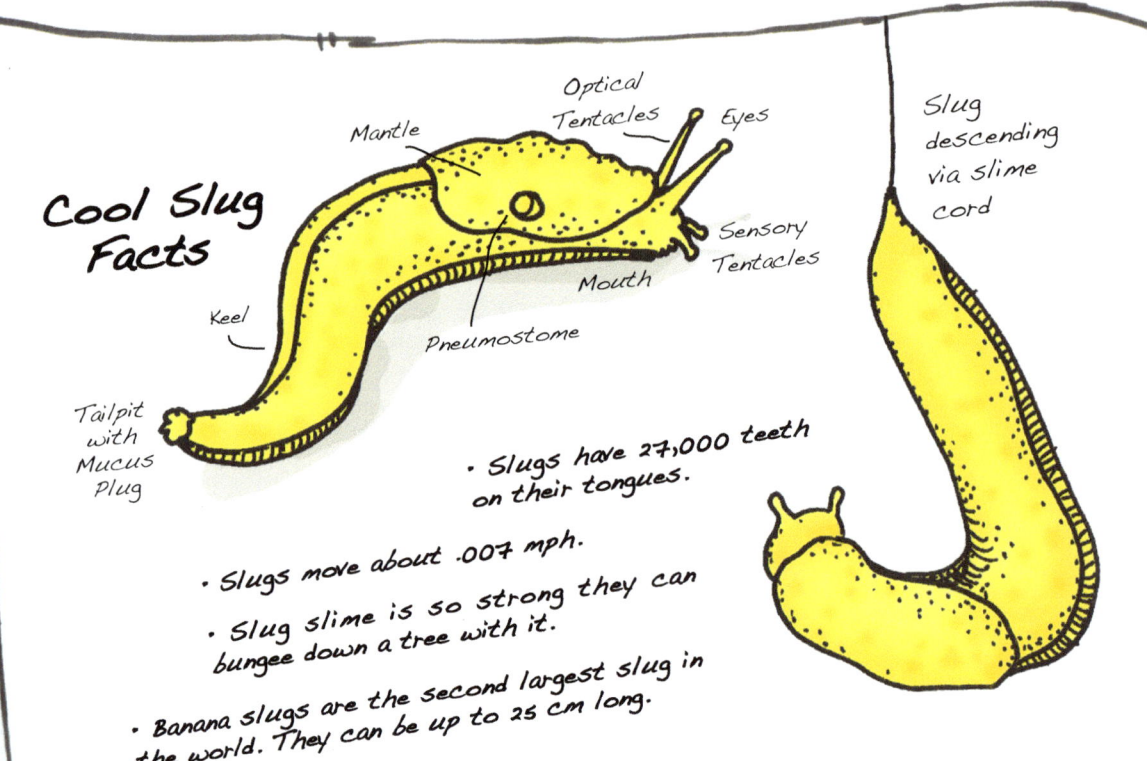

Mantle

Optical Tentacles

Eyes

Keel

Pneumostome

Mouth

Sensory Tentacles

Tailpit with Mucus Plug

Slug descending via slime cord

- Slugs have 27,000 teeth on their tongues.

- Slugs move about .007 mph.

- Slug slime is so strong they can bungee down a tree with it.

- Banana slugs are the second largest slug in the world. They can be up to 25 cm long.

Glossary

Community: A group of organisms in a specific habitat that grow or live together.

Consumers: Organisms that get their energy by eating other living things. Examples include animals, fungi, and bacteria.

Decomposers: Organisms that play the important role of breaking down dead animals and plants, which returns nutrients to the soil. Examples include insects, bacteria, and fungi.

Ecology: The study of the interactions between organisms and their environment.

Ecosystem: A group of organisms that interact with their specific non-living environment.

Gastropod: Gastro refers to stomach; pod refers to foot. A scientific classification of animals that includes slugs, snails, sea slugs, and limpets.

Habitat: An organism's home.

Naturalist: Someone who learns and teaches about the natural world.

Niche: The specific role or job a plant or animal has within its community.

Organism: A specific animal, plant, or single-celled life form.

Photosynthesis: The process in which plants combine light energy from the sun with carbon dioxide and water to produce glucose and oxygen.

Producers: Organisms that use the sun's energy to produce new living material through photosynthesis. Producers form the basis of food chains.